WORLD ENERGY ISSUES

NUCLEAR POWER
Is It Too Risky?

JIM PIPE

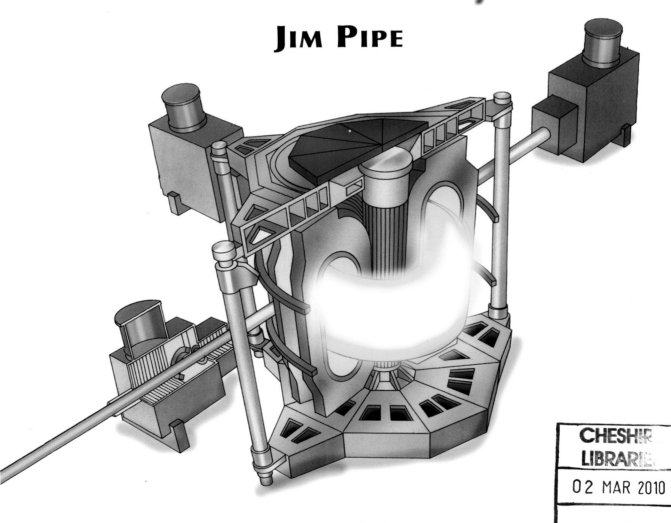

ALADDIN/WATTS
LONDON • SYDNEY

Contents

© Aladdin Books Ltd 2010

Designed and produced by
Aladdin Books Ltd
PO Box 53987
London SW15 2SF

First published in 2010
by Franklin Watts
338 Euston Road
London NW1 3BH

Franklin Watts Australia
Level 17/207 Kent Street
Sydney NSW 2000

Franklin Watts is a division of
Hachette Children's Books,
an Hachette UK company.
www.hachette.co.uk

All rights reserved
Printed in Malaysia

Scientific consultant: Rob Bowden

A catalogue record for
this book is available
from the British Library.

Dewey Classification:
333.792'4

ISBN 978 07496 9080 9

What's the Issue?

⚠ **Radiation Risk**
Unlike other forms of energy, nuclear power produces dangerous radiation as well as heat.

Today, there is a growing demand for energy, especially electricity. Most of our energy comes from fossil fuels such as oil, gas and coal. However, burning fossil fuels releases gases that add to global warming. Oil may also run out in the next 60 years. The challenge is to find a reliable alternative without adding to our environmental problems.

Using nuclear power in the next few decades could help to slow climate change, giving scientists time to develop renewable energy sources such as solar power, wind power and biofuels.

Nuclear power, however, brings its own problems – nuclear plants are expensive to build and no one has solved how to get rid of nuclear waste. There is also the risk of a nuclear accident.

▼ **Nuclear Power Plant Control Room**

3

Why Nuclear?

When the first nuclear power stations were built in the 1950s, they were seen as the future of energy. But after an accident at the US Three Mile Island reactor in 1979 and the horrific Chernobyl disaster in 1986, many people no longer trusted nuclear power. As a result, most power stations built in the last 20 years run on coal, oil and gas.

Burning these fossil fuels releases the "greenhouse gases" that are blamed for global warming, which scientists predict will lead to floods, droughts and rising sea levels. Nuclear plants do not give off these gases, one reason why the UK and the United States plan to build more of them. The new plants should be safer and use fuel more efficiently – but dealing with dangerous nuclear waste remains a problem.

◖ Dirty Power

Coal-fired power plants in the United States alone release 10 per cent of the world's carbon dioxide, a major greenhouse gas.

Nuclear Power: For

• Nuclear power plants produce far fewer greenhouse gases than power plants that burn fossil fuels such as coal and oil.

• Once built, nuclear plants provide a cheap source of electricity.

• Modern nuclear plants can provide power almost 24 hours a day, seven days a week, unlike wind and solar power.

• Nuclear power can also be used to create the hydrogen needed for fuel cells, a possible power source for cars of the future (and one that reduces greenhouses gases).

Nuclear Power: Against

• Nuclear power plants are expensive to build.

• Nuclear power is not a renewable source of energy as there are only limited supplies of uranium, the main fuel used in nuclear reactors.

• The radioactive waste created by nuclear reactors must be buried deep underground for thousands of years.

• There is a risk of a nuclear disaster. A bad accident could kill or injure thousands of people.

• Countries that can refine uranium for power stations can also use it to make nuclear weapons.

• Nuclear reactors release small amounts of radioactive gases (but so do coal-fired power stations).

• The cooling systems in many nuclear plants use two-and-a-half times as much water as fossil fuel plants.

✷ Building a Reactor

Nuclear energy is too dangerous to use in cars or homes. It requires complex technology to safely control atomic reactions, and thick shields to protect from radioactive waste.

What Is Nuclear Power?

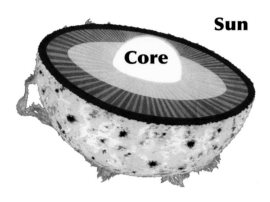

Sun

Core

⚛ What Are Atoms?

Every object in the world is made up of tiny particles called atoms. These are the basic building blocks of the universe.

Everything from a tiny hair to the Sun's fireball is made from atoms. In fact, the Sun's heat and light are caused by a giant nuclear reaction inside the Sun's core.

Nuclear power is a type of energy. There are many sources of energy, such as the petrol burnt in car engines or coal burnt to release heat energy. Nuclear power is the heat energy released when certain kinds of atoms are split. This heat is used to boil water and create steam, which drives turbines that generate electricity.

When you turn on lights or machines in your home, you may be using the electricity created by nuclear power. Nuclear energy has also been used to power ships and submarines, while nuclear substances are used in weapons and medical equipment.

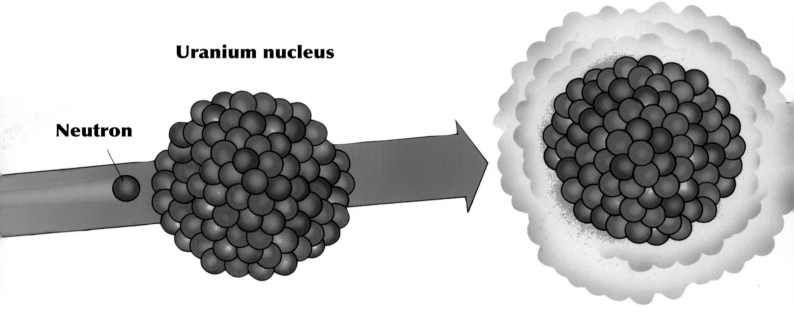

Neutron strikes nucleus

Uranium nucleus

Neutron

How Fission Works

1 *A neutron is fired at a uranium atom.*

2 *The neutron strikes the unstable uranium nucleus.*

🕙 Inside Atoms

Nuclear power comes from the energy stored in atoms. The central part of an atom is the nucleus, which gives us the word nuclear. Each nucleus contains smaller particles called protons and neutrons. Smaller particles, called electrons, circle around the nucleus.

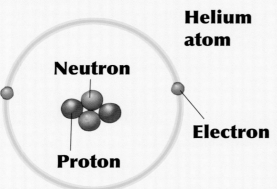

Helium atom

Neutron

Electron

Proton

🕙 Splitting Atoms – Fission

In 1939, scientists discovered that the unstable atoms of a metal called uranium could be split in two, creating enormous amounts of energy. This is called nuclear fission.

During fission, atoms throw out even smaller particles called neutrons. These smash into other atoms and break them apart, causing a chain reaction as more and more atoms are split in two. This is what happens inside the reactor of a nuclear power station.

Nucleus splits in two, releasing neutrons

Heat and radiation are released

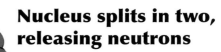

Reaction continues

3 *The uranium nucleus splits into lighter nuclei and free neutrons.*

4 *The free neutrons crash into other uranium atoms, causing a "chain reaction".*

Working with Atoms

Late in the 19th century, scientists discovered that the atoms of certain elements give off invisible particles and rays, known as radiation. This discovery led to the development of nuclear energy in the 20th century. On 16 July 1945, the first atomic weapon was tested, showing the awesome power of the atom. Later that year, two bombs were dropped on the Japanese cities of Hiroshima and Nagasaki, killing over 220,000 people.

The radiation caused by nuclear fission in a power station is also very dangerous – it can kill or injure. To protect workers, many operations inside a reactor are carried out by remote control, and instruments warn against high radiation levels.

☢ Exploding Stars

Scientists believe uranium was formed when stars exploded over six billion years ago. Uranium's radioactivity provides some of the heat inside the Earth.

What Is Radioactivity?

The word radioactive means "giving off rays". It is used to describe unstable atoms, such as uranium atoms, that naturally give off rays. These rays cannot be seen, smelt or touched, but they are dangerous and can cause serious illnesses such as cancer.

Nuclear Explosion

In a nuclear bomb, the chain reaction is not controlled as it is inside a nuclear reactor. The chain reaction grows bigger and bigger, giving off an enormous amount of energy in one go as a nuclear explosion.

⊽ Anti-radiation suits *are worn in areas with high radiation. The worker on the right is using a geiger counter to measure the radiation.*

Working Safely

The people who work in a nuclear power station must be protected. They wear radiation-resistant clothes and are checked to make sure their radiation levels are safe. Precise tools handle radioactive material by remote control.

ENERGY FACTS: Nuclear Timeline

1896 French scientist Henri Becquerel discovers radioactivity when invisible rays from uranium make a photographic plate go dark.
1898 Polish-born French physicist Marie Curie finds two new elements: polonium and radium.
1899 British scientist Ernest Rutherford finds that uranium gives off different kinds of rays. He later discovers that atoms have a nucleus.
1905 Albert Einstein works out that when a nucleus breaks up, some of its tiny mass turns into huge amounts of energy.
1938 A uranium atom is first split in the Berlin laboratory of Otto Hahn.
1942 Enrico Fermi leads the US team that produces the first successful chain reaction.
1951 Electricity is generated for the first time at the EBR-I nuclear reactor in Idaho, USA.
1953 Work begins on world's first nuclear power station: Calder Hall plant in the UK.
1960s-2009 Global nuclear energy production rises from less than 1 gigawatt (GW) in 1960 to 372 GW in 2009.

Alpha particle

Beta particle

Nucleus

Gamma ray

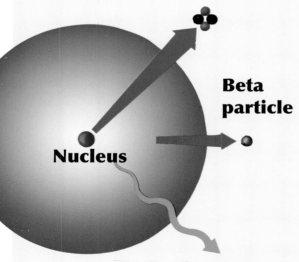

Types of Radiation

Radioactive materials give off three kinds of rays:
1 *Alpha particles (protons and neutrons) can be stopped by a sheet a paper.*
2 *Beta particles (electrons) can be stopped by a sheet of aluminium 3 mm thick.*
3 *Gamma rays (waves) need a thick sheet of lead or a concrete shield over 2 metres thick to stop them.*

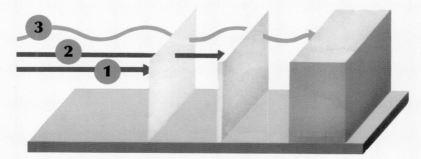

Nuclear Fuels

Uranium, the fuel used to produce nuclear power, is a heavy, silver-white metal found in ores (rocks that contain metals) such as pitchblende, sandstone and granite. Some 40,000 tonnes of uranium are mined every year, over half of it in just three countries: Canada, Australia and Kazakhstan.

The metal is removed from the ore using acid. However, the uranium found in nature is not all of one kind; it is a mix of different forms known as isotopes. One isotope, uranium 235 (or U-235), works best for nuclear fission, so the natural uranium must be purified to increase the amount of U-235.

☯ Step 1: Mining the Ore

Most uranium ore is not very radioactive so it is often mined at the surface in strip mines. Here the layer of soil over the ore is removed with giant scrapers. This uncovers the ore, which is then dug out and carried away.

ENERGY FACTS: Uranium 235

The isotope (form) of uranium used in nuclear fission is known as U-235 because it has 92 protons and 143 neutrons in its nucleus (92 + 143 = 235).

This isotope is very unstable and releases the most energy when its nucleus breaks apart.

Underground Mines

When mining uranium, great care is taken so that workers are not exposed to radiation or the dangerous chemicals used to remove uranium from the ore.

In some underground mines, the ore is cut from the rock by remote-control drills so that no workers come into contact with the radioactive ore.

Old Uranium Mine
The radioactive waste in some mines can pose a risk for up to 250,000 years after the mine is closed.

Step 2: From Ore to Oxide

The mined uranium ore is crushed, ground up and treated with chemicals. Sulphuric acid is often used to remove the radium that makes the uranium ore so radioactive. The end result is mostly uranium oxide, known as "yellowcake", which is dried and then packed into drums for shipment.

Yellowcake

Isotopes

Isotopes are different forms of the same element. For example, there are three forms of hydrogen:

1 *The ordinary hydrogen atom (found in water) has one proton and electron.*

2 *Deuterium also has a neutron in its nucleus.*

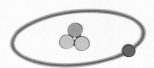

3 *Tritium has two neutrons in its nucleus.*

Step 3: Enriching the Uranium

The uranium oxide cannot be used in nuclear power stations as fuel. First it must be purified, or "enriched", by increasing the amount of the isotope U-235 from 1 to 3 per cent. This is done by turning the uranium into a gas and filtering it, or by whirling the uranium around in a machine called a centrifuge.

◑ Bundles of fuel rods

contain some 180 to 265 fuel rods.

◐ Step 4: Fuel Rods

The enriched uranium is then heated into small pellets of uranium oxide. The pellets are packed into stainless steel tubes about 4 m long to form fuel rods, or fuel pins. These are placed into bundles ready for use in nuclear power stations.

◑ Fuel from Weapons

An important source of uranium is the world's stockpile of nuclear weapons. In a deal signed with Russia in 1993, the United States agreed to buy 500 tonnes of uranium from nuclear warheads every year for 20 years. The uranium may only be used for non-military purposes.

The same powerful explosion that occurs in an atomic explosion also powers nuclear reactors, but here fission is controlled so it occurs slowly. Fission takes place in the centre of the reactor, known as the core, which contains the fuel rods. Around these flow a coolant, either water or gas.

The coolant carries the heat given off by the rods to a steam generator. Here it is used to boil water to steam. The steam is then blasted against giant turbine blades. As these turn, they drive generators, which produce electricity.

A Controlled Reaction

The reaction is controlled in two main ways. The neutrons created by fission move very fast, so they are slowed down by a moderator, usually water or carbon.

Control rods, made of boron or cadmium, also absorb some of the neutrons. Raising or lowering the rods allows engineers to speed up or slow down the nuclear reaction.

Inside the Reactor Core

1 *Rods of nuclear fuel contain only small amounts of uranium (U-235), to help control the size of the chain reaction.*

2 *Nuclear fission occurs: neutrons crash into uranium atoms, releasing two or three more neutrons which smash into other U-235 atoms, creating a chain reaction.*

3 *The fuel rods are surrounded by a coolant, usually water or gas, which also acts as a "moderator".*

4 *Control rods absorb some of the neutrons.*

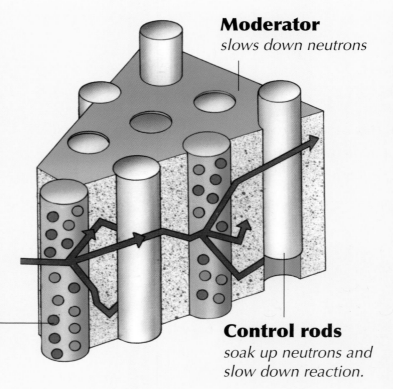

Moderator
slows down neutrons

Fuel rods
where fission takes place

Control rods
soak up neutrons and slow down reaction.

Reactor

The fuel rods are lowered into a large tank of water, the coolant. Without this, the burning rods would melt.

5 *Fission heats up the coolant water to temperatures of over 300 °C. The water does not boil because the reactor core is kept under very high pressure.*

6 *This superhot coolant runs down a pipe into the steam generator. The hot pipe works like the element in a kettle, and heats a separate tank of clean water inside the steam generator.*

7 *When this water turns to steam, it turns the turbines.*

8 *The steam is cooled with water from the cooling tower in the condenser. It turns back into water and is used again in the steam generator.*

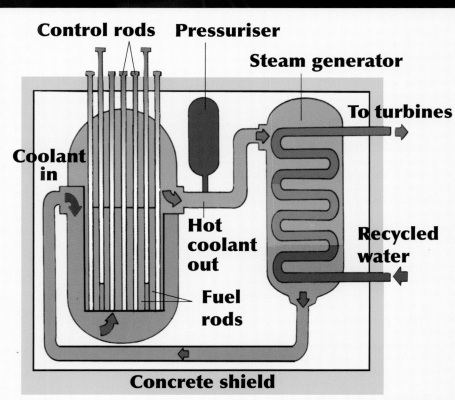

Control rods Pressuriser
Steam generator
To turbines
Coolant in
Hot coolant out
Fuel rods
Recycled water
Concrete shield

A Nuclear Power Station

Over half the nuclear reactors in the world are pressurised water reactors (PWRs), which use water as a coolant and a moderator. A typical PWR has a core about 13 m tall, made of steel some 23 cm thick, and contains some 200-300 bundles of fuel rods. The rods last around one year before they need to be replaced. In case there is a leak, the reactor core and the steam generator are contained in a metre-thick concrete and steel dome, the containment building.

Steam goes from the steam generator to the turbines to generate electricity. Transformers convert the electricity into a high voltage, so power lines can carry it more efficiently over long distances.

⚠ **PWRs** *are often built close to rivers, lakes or the sea for a good supply of water. They can have a big impact on local wildlife. This plant at San Onofre, California, USA, sucks in an estimated 500 tonnes of fish each year.*

Running a Plant

A nuclear plant costs a lot to build but is cheap to run, so it makes sense to operate it 24 hours a day, seven days a week. In practice, however, this can be hard to achieve due to unexpected breakdowns.

Twenty years ago most nuclear plants ran for 60 to 70 per cent of the time. Thanks to experience and better controls, many plants today are 90 per cent efficient. Some can be refuelled without being stopped.

Inside a Pressurised Water Reactor (PWR)

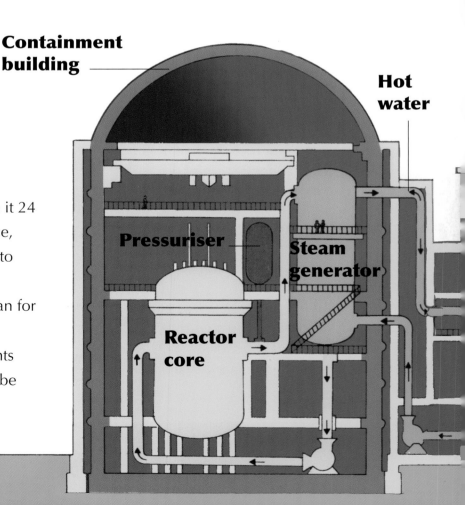

Containment building

Hot water

Pressuriser

Steam generator

Reactor core

Control Room

Operations in a nuclear power plant are monitored in a central control room, both by computers and by experienced controllers who constantly check what is happening inside the reactor. If there is an emergency, computers shut down the reactor.

How a Generator Works

In 1831, British scientist Michael Faraday found that you can create electricity by moving a magnet through a coil of copper wire. Inside a generator, the shaft makes magnets spin inside wire coils, producing electricity in the same way.

Turbine
blades turned by steam.

Generator
magnets spin inside coil.

Emergencies

One of the biggest dangers with a PWR is that the cooling water might get blocked or lost. The reactor then immediately shuts itself down and the emergency core-cooling system comes into operation. This floods the core with cold water to prevent overheating.

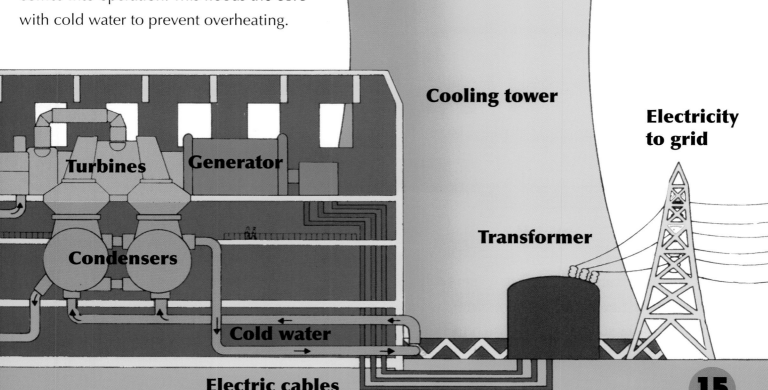

Cooling tower

Electricity to grid

Turbines

Generator

Condensers

Transformer

Cold water

Electric cables

Types of Reactor

Nuclear energy can be used to power different types of reactors. While PWRs use water as a moderator and coolant, others use gas or graphite (carbon). Fast breeder reactors can produce power and nuclear fuel at the same time. In India, scientists are working on a reactor that uses thorium to "breed" (make) uranium.

Nuclear reactors are also used to power submarines and ships such as aircraft carriers and ice-breakers. However, reactors are too dangerous to use in road vehicles where accidents are common.

⬢ Gas-cooled Reactors

Gas-cooled reactors (GCRs) use the gases carbon dioxide or helium as a coolant instead of water, and the fuel rods are surrounded by a graphite (carbon) moderator. Carbon dioxide is used in gas-cooled nuclear plants in the UK and France.

⬢ Research Reactor

The Swiss CROCUS reactor is used for teaching reactor physics. Its low power means that within a few hours of shutdown, it is safe for scientists to enter the reactor.

AGRs

Torness nuclear power station in Scotland has two advanced gas-cooled reactors (AGRs). It was built in 1988.

Fast Breeder Reactors

A breeder reactor creates new fuel faster than it uses it. This fuel can then be used in other reactors. Such reactors are also called "fast" because they do not slow down the neutrons during fission. However, there have been problems with fast breeders. Some experts argue they are more dangerous than other power stations. Today, the only fast breeder reactor in use is the Super Phoenix in France.

Nuclear-powered submarine

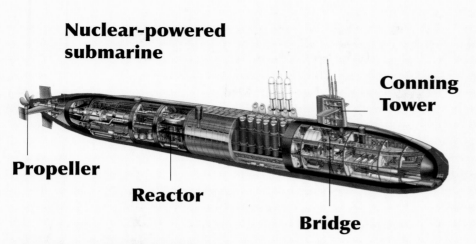

Conning Tower

Propeller

Reactor

Bridge

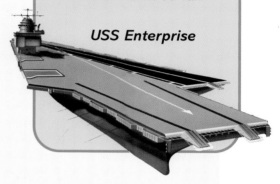
Nuclear Propulsion

Nuclear submarines are powered by small pressurised water reactors (PWRs). The reactor creates steam which drives a turbine. This is connected to a propeller shaft which pushes the vessel through the water. The reactor can run for seven years without refuelling, and as 1 kg of uranium produces so much energy, it allows a submarine to stay underwater for months at a time.

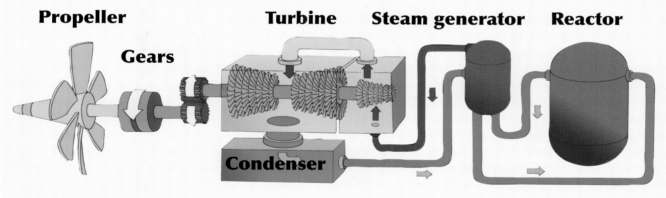

Propeller **Gears** **Turbine** **Steam generator** **Reactor**

Condenser

⊙ Thorium Reactors

Future breeder reactors may run on thorium, which is more common and less radioactive than uranium.

To kickstart fission, the thorium is hit by neutrons fired at it by a device called a particle accelerator. The neutrons cause the thorium to turn into uranium.

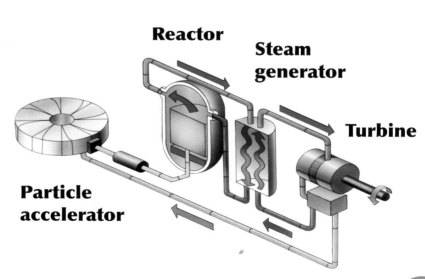

Reactor

Steam generator

Turbine

Particle accelerator

A Nuclear Future?

The amount of energy the world uses is rising. Meanwhile, coal- and oil-burning power stations across the globe are spewing billions of tonnes of the global-warming gas carbon dioxide into the atmosphere every year. Developing nations, such as India and China, are also building new coal plants at a rapid rate. However, they are also planning a new generation of nuclear power plants, which could help to slow global warming.

Though renewable energy sources such as wind and solar power are clean and work well, they cannot yet provide constant power or a surge in power during peak hours.

Replacing Fossil Fuels

Burning fossil fuels such as coal, oil and gas contributes to climate change – the carbon dioxide they produce acts like a giant window trapping the Sun's heat and pushing up temperatures. Most scientists predict that global warming will have very damaging effects, such as rising sea levels, flooding, droughts and an increase in hurricanes. By comparison, nuclear power plants release less than 1 per cent of the carbon dioxide gas produced by coal-fired power stations.

Daya Bay
Nuclear Plant

Power for All?

Several Asian countries are building new nuclear power plants in the next 10 years: China (30 reactors), India (10 reactors) and Japan (13 reactors). However, the United States and other nuclear powers are worried that some developing countries might use the technology to build nuclear weapons.

☯ Nuclear Plans

China currently has 11 nuclear reactors, including two at Daya Bay (pictured below). However, it plans to build 100 more, producing 300,000 megawatts (MW) by 2050.

Large Energy Output

Once a nuclear plant is up and running, it can produce huge amounts of energy from small amounts of fuel. The reactor in a nuclear power station big enough to supply a city of 1 million people burns just 3 kg of fuel (uranium) each day. It would take many hectares of land covered with solar collectors or wind farms to supply the same power.

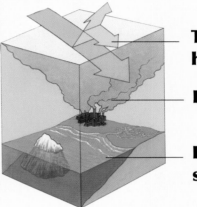

Sunlight

Trapped heat

Pollution

Rising sea levels

Global warming *is caused by man-made gases which trap the Sun's heat in the atmosphere. Because they work like the glass in a greenhouse, they are known as "greenhouse" gases.*

What Are the Risks?

Radiation symbol

If nuclear energy has some big advantages over fossil fuels and renewables, why aren't there more nuclear reactors? In fact, countries such as Germany are currently shutting down reactors faster than they are building them.

The main reason is that many people don't trust the safety of nuclear power and the radioactive waste that it creates. Though only two serious nuclear accidents have occurred, at Chernobyl and Three Mile Island, another bad accident could affect thousands of people.

▷ Three Mile Island Accident

The worst fear of a nuclear plant designer is that a "meltdown" occurs. Here the hot fuel burns its way through the bottom of a reactor and into the ground. This almost happened in an accident at the Three Mile Island plant, Pennsylvania, USA, on 28 March 1979. Luckily, the accident was brought under control. Though nobody was hurt, the accident forced the US government to cancel many new nuclear power stations.

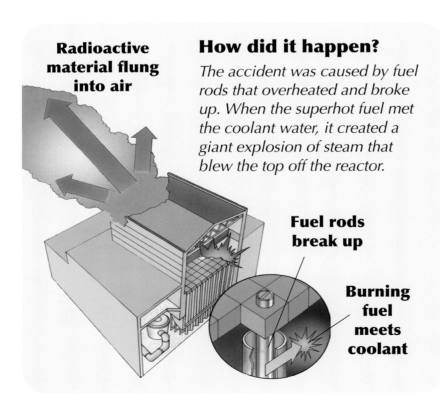

Radioactive material flung into air

How did it happen?

The accident was caused by fuel rods that overheated and broke up. When the superhot fuel met the coolant water, it created a giant explosion of steam that blew the top off the reactor.

Fuel rods break up

Burning fuel meets coolant

◁ Chernobyl Disaster

In April 1986, the Chernobyl power station in the Ukraine (then part of the Soviet Union) was ripped apart by an enormous explosion. Helicopters were used to "bomb" the reactor with a mixture of sand, clay, lead and boron. It took two weeks to put out the fire and stop the reaction.

Forty-seven staff and firefighters died (28 from radiation exposure), and another 130,000 people got high radiation doses. Harmful gases leaked out into the air, and the fields for 500 sq km around were contaminated.

Dealing with Waste

Though nuclear reactors can produce cheap energy, it takes a lot of energy and money to clean up the waste they create. After the used fuel rods have been reprocessed, the remaining radioactive waste is so dangerous it cannot just be thrown away.

There is no way to deal with it apart from burying it and waiting for 10,000 years. Today, most waste is being held at temporary sites until a long-term solution to the problem can be found. These sites, many deep underground, have to be managed and kept cool to prevent fire and leaks.

The Fuel Cycle

In some countries, used fuel rods are taken to a reprocessing plant after they have been removed from the reactor. In the reprocessing plant, the fuel rods are dissolved in acid and the uranium is recovered and made into new fuel rods. Plutonium is also created. This can be used as fuel for fast breeder reactors.

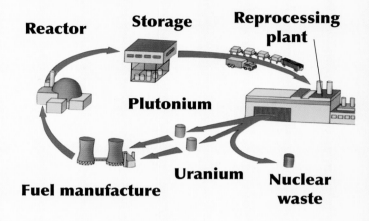

Reactor   Storage   Reprocessing plant

Plutonium

Fuel manufacture   Uranium   Nuclear waste

Underground Storage

Even if a long-term solution is found for storing nuclear waste, it will need to be safe from terrorists who could use it to build a "dirty" nuclear bomb.

Storage Pools

Used fuel rods are temporarily stored in pools of water before being buried or recycled.

Laser beams · Main laser · Laser beams · Fuel pellet

Laser Fusion

US scientists have tried using a laser-driven reactor to produce fusion. Tiny pellets of nuclear fuel are blasted by laser beams for just a billionth of a second, creating the temperatures needed for fusion.

◗ Tokamak

This Russian test fusion reactor is known as a Tokamak. Named after its doughnut-shaped container, it can produce a temperature of 510 million °C. The Tokamak uses magnetic and electric fields to heat and squeeze hydrogen plasma. This creates a fusion reaction that could one day generate electricity.

What Is Plasma?

When a gas such as hydrogen gets extremely hot, its atoms lose all their electrons, leaving a cloud of nuclei and free-floating electrons. This is called plasma. When hydrogen becomes plasma, it can conduct electricity very well and can be squeezed by the electromagnets in a Tokamak.

Nuclear Fusion

In fission, atoms produce heat energy when they break up. Energy is also produced when atoms join up. This is called fusion. In a fusion reactor, hydrogen atoms come together to form helium atoms, neutrons and vast amounts of energy. It's the same reaction that powers hydrogen bombs and the Sun.

It takes incredibly high temperatures for fusion to happen, and so far no one has found a way to sustain them. Though there are several experimental fusion reactors around the world, it may be 40 years before the technology can be used to generate large amounts of electricity.

Vacuum chamber
holds the plasma.

Magnets
squeeze the plasma.

Plasma

Heat exchanger
makes steam to turn turbines.

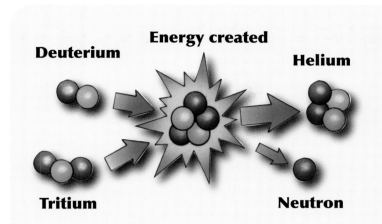

Deuterium

Energy created

Helium

Tritium

Neutron

Creating Fusion

One of the most common ways to create fusion uses deuterium and tritium, two isotopes of hydrogen. When these combine, they form a helium atom and a neutron, while giving off vast amounts of energy.

While uranium is relatively rare, deuterium can be extracted from seawater and tritium from lithium found in the Earth's crust.

Limitless Power

If fusion were achieved on Earth, almost limitless energy would be available. The fusion of 1 kg of nuclei would release more energy than burning 18 million kg of coal. The other advantage is that nuclear fusion produces only small amounts of radioactive waste.

◐ Star Fusion

Nuclear fusion is what powers stars like our Sun. At its core, the high temperatures (15 million °C) and the force of gravity squeezing atoms together cause hydrogen nuclei to turn into helium nuclei, producing enormous amounts of energy that light and heat our planet, 150 million km away!

ENERGY FACTS: What's Needed for Fusion to Work?

Heat – The heat needed to start fusion is at least 50 million °C. Though a nuclear bomb can create this amount of heat, a way needs to be found without blowing the power plant up!

Pressure – To make hydrogen atoms fuse, they must be squeezed close together by using incredibly strong magnetic and electric fields or powerful lasers.

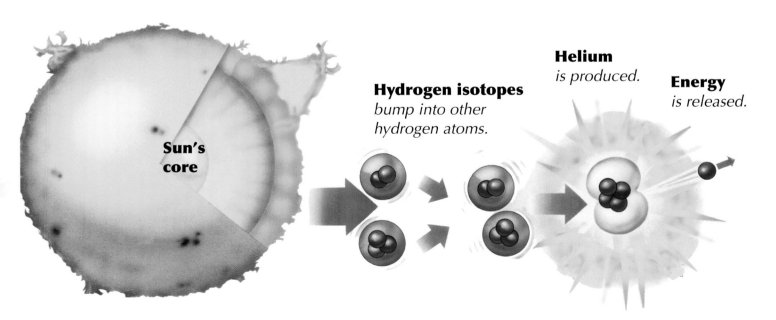

Sun's core

Hydrogen isotopes *bump into other hydrogen atoms.*

Helium *is produced.*

Energy *is released.*

New Designs

⚠ Building a Plant

A third-generation European Pressurised Reactor (EPR) is being built at Olkiluoto, Finland. It should be in operation by 2012.

The best hope for a nuclear future lies in new designs for reactors. In 20 to 30 years' time, fourth-generation machines could work at much higher temperatures and get far more energy from each kilogram of uranium. They would also produce less toxic waste. With simpler safety features, they could cool themselves down in the event of an accident, making them less tempting targets for terrorists.

Yet nuclear plants are so expensive that many countries can't afford them. While nuclear power offers a cleaner alternative to fossil fuels, in the long term the world needs to develop renewable alternatives such as biofuels and wind power.

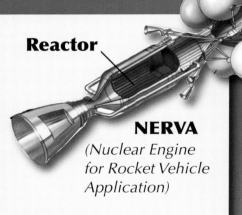

Reactor

NERVA
(Nuclear Engine for Rocket Vehicle Application)

Nuclear Rockets

NASA is currently looking into developing a nuclear thermal rocket (NTR) to power deep-space rockets. During the 1960s, NASA scientists attempted to build a nuclear rocket that would carry astronauts to Mars (called NERVA) using hydrogen gas pumped into a white-hot nuclear reactor.

Fusion – A Future Hope?

Nuclear fusion could provide a safe, clean energy source for future generations with several advantages over current fission reactors:

- *Good fuel supply – deuterium and tritium are more common than uranium.*
- *Safer – fusion reactors will make less radiation than the natural background radiation we live with in our daily lives.*
- *Less waste – fusion reactors will not produce the same high-level nuclear wastes as fission reactors.*
- *Less danger – fusion reactors can't be used to make nuclear weapons.*

◐ Third-generation Power Plants

The latest designs for nuclear power stations such as the ESBWR (Economic Simplified Boiling Water Reactor) are cheaper, simpler and safer. Above the reactor are large tanks of water that flood the reactor if sensors detect that the water levels have become too low. Known as a gravity driven cooling system (GDCS), this can keep the reactor stable without needing pumps or a command from an operator.

◑ Nuclear plant

Older plants such as this one may be replaced in the next 20 years by a new generation of reactors.

Safety system

Turbines

Reactor

Control Room

ESBWR
(Economic Simplified Boiling Water Reactor)

Producing Hydrogen

Like other forms of energy that produce electricity, nuclear power could be used to produce hydrogen. In the future this may be used as a fuel in cars as oil gets increasingly expensive or eventually runs out.

Pebble-bed Reactors

In China, scientists are building a pebble-bed reactor that is small enough to be assembled from mass-produced parts. The reactor is powered by 27,000 snooker-sized graphite balls packed with tiny flecks of uranium fuel. The gas helium is used as a coolant. This can reach much higher temperatures without bursting the pipes, so there is almost no danger of a meltdown. Using helium instead of water also makes these reactors a lot cheaper as there is no need for an expensive cooling system or containment building.

Uranium

"Pebble" fuel

Graphite shell

HOT OFF THE PRESS

Safe from attack?

■ In 2012, construction will start on a new European Pressurised Reactor (EPR) in France.

This third-generation nuclear power plant has several different safety measures, including four independent emergency cooling systems, leaktight containment around the reactor, and a two-layer 2.6-m-thick concrete wall designed to be strong enough to withstand a direct hit from a terrorist aeroplane.

There are also plans to build EPRs in Abu Dhabi, China, India and Italy.

The European Pressurised Reactor (EPR) currently being built in France

A future for fusion?

■ The very latest in fusion technology is the International Thermonuclear Experimental Reactor. Known as ITER, it is currently being built in Cadarache, France, in a collaboration between the European Union, the United States, Japan, China, India, Russia and South Korea.

The project hopes that its fusion reactor, based on a Tokamak (see page 22), can be used to make electricity on a large scale. It will weigh 23,000 tonnes – the same as three Eiffel Towers.

It is designed to produce around 500 megawatts of fusion power for up to 1,000 seconds. The reactor will take nearly 10 years to build and is scheduled to be switched on in 2018.

The ITER Tokamak complex is now being built on a platform one kilometre long by 400 metres wide.

A final voyage

■ The world's first nuclear-powered surface ship, the *Lenin*, made its final voyage in 2009.

Launched in 1957, the Russian icebreaker weighed 16,000 tonnes and was powered by three PWRs. When an accident occurred in 1967, explosives were used to cut the reactor away.

Demolition likely for older plants

■ In the next 20 years many older nuclear plants will need to be shut down.

What does it take to tear down an outdated plant? In 2007, a US demolition team used 4,400 dynamite charges to bring down four outdated nuclear cooling towers at Sellafield in the UK. One tower was just 40m away from a nuclear fuel processing plant.

The weight of each tower shell was 5,200 tonnes and it took 12 weeks to remove the rubble. RDX, a special high-velocity explosive was used to cut through the steel.

The destruction of the four towers was the first step to decommission the Calder Hall site, made up of 62 buildings.

The Galileo probe passing Jupiter

Nuclear fuel for spacecraft likely to run out

■ The amazing pictures of the outer solar system taken by the Galileo and Cassini spacecraft were powered by the nuclear isotope plutonium 238. Over 50 years ago, NASA developed radioisotope thermal generators (RTGs) that convert the heat from radioactive decay into electricity. They're the only long-term source of power available when light

" Within 8 years, the fuel needed for missions such as the Mars Science Laboratory may run out. "

from the Sun is too weak to use solar cells. The reactors that produced the plutonium 238 were shut down 20 years ago. Within 8 years, the fuel needed for missions such as the Mars Science Laboratory may run out, unless equipment is built to process it.

Giant fusion laser

■ A new giant laser is currently being tested at the Lawrence Livermoore Laboratory near San Francisco, California, USA. The same size as a stadium, it has 192 separate beams that combine into one huge beam with the same heat energy as the Sun itself! The laser will be used to explore fusion and one day could find a way to create huge amounts of electricity.

How long will today's uranium reserves last?

■ The reserves of uranium ore are expected to last about 100 years. The largest uranium mine in the world today is Olympic Dam in South Australia.

It is currently being enlarged and by 2013, it will mine 19,000 tonnes of uranium oxide each year.

How Nuclear Compares

While fossil fuels are cheap, they release carbon dioxide into the atmosphere, causing pollution and global warming. Renewable energy will reduce this problem, but in the short term it may not be able to supply more than 20 per cent of our needs. Nuclear power could provide us with the extra power, but reactors are very expensive and take years to build.

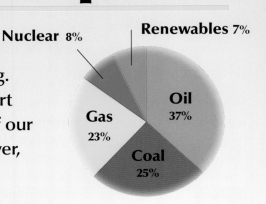

Nuclear 8% **Renewables** 7%
Oil 37%
Gas 23%
Coal 25%

World Energy Sources

NON-RENEWABLE ENERGY

Nuclear

For:
Nuclear power is constant and reliable, and doesn't contribute to global warming.

Against:
Not renewable as uranium (the main nuclear fuel) will eventually run out. Nuclear waste is so dangerous it must be buried for thousands of years. Also the risk of a nuclear accident.

Gas

For:
Gas is relatively cheap, and produces less greenhouses gases than oil and coal.

Against:
Burning gas releases carbon dioxide. Gas is not renewable and the world's natural gas reserves are limited. Gas pipelines can disrupt the migration routes of animals such as caribou.

Coal

For:
Coal is cheap and supplies of coal are expected to last another 150 years.

Against:
Coal-fired power stations give off the most greenhouse gases. They also produce sulphur dioxide, creating acid rain. Coal mining can be very destructive to the landscape.

Oil

For:
Oil is cheap and easy to store, transport and use.

Against:
Oil is not renewable and it is getting more expensive to get out of the ground. Burning oil releases large amounts of greenhouse gases. Oil spills, especially at sea, cause severe pollution.

RENEWABLE ENERGY

Wind Power

For:

Wind power needs no fuel, it's renewable and doesn't pollute.

Against:

Wind is unpredictable, so wind farms need a back-up power supply. Possible danger to bird flocks. It takes thousands of wind turbines to produce the same power as a nuclear plant.

Solar Power

For:

Solar power needs no fuel, it's renewable and doesn't pollute.

Against:

Solar power stations are very expensive as solar (photovoltaic) cells cost a lot compared to the amount of electricity they produce. They're unreliable unless used in a very sunny climate.

Hydroelectric Power

For:

Hydroelectric power needs no fuel, is renewable and doesn't pollute.

Against:

Hydroelectric power is very expensive to build. A large dam will flood a very large area upstream, impacting on animals and people there. A dam can affect water quality downstream.

Geothermal Power

For:

Geothermal power needs no fuel, it's renewable and doesn't pollute.

Against:

There aren't many suitable places for a geothermal power station as you need hot rocks of the right type and not too deep. It can "run out of steam". Underground poisonous gases can be a danger.

Biofuels

For:

Biofuels are cheap and renewable and can be made from waste.

Against:

Growing biofuels from energy crops reduces the land available for food and uses up vital resources such as fresh water. Like fossil fuels, biofuels can produce greenhouse gases.

Tidal Power

For:

Tidal power needs no fuel, is reliable, renewable and doesn't pollute.

Against:

Tidal power machines are expensive to build and only provide power for around 10 hours each day, when the tide is actually moving in or out. Not an efficient way of producing electricity.

Glossary and Resources

chain reaction A series of continuing reactions in which one causes the next.

control rods Inside a nuclear reactor, control rods made of cadmium or boron are used to slow down or speed up the reaction taking place.

coolant Gas or liquid that takes heat away from a reactor.

core The central part of a reactor where fuel is turned into energy.

electron The particle which circles the nucleus of an atom. When electrons are caused by radioactive decay, they are called beta particles.

element A substance that cannot be made into a simpler form.

fast breeder A reactor that makes more fuel than it uses and does not slow down neutrons during fission. Most fast breeders turn uranium 238 into plutonium 239.

fission The splitting of an atom into smaller parts, which releases energy.

fuel enrichment Increasing the amount of uranium 235 isotope in nuclear fuel so it is concentrated enough for use in nuclear reactors.

fusion Joining two nuclei together, which creates energy.

generator A machine that creates electricity from mechanical energy.

isotopes Different forms of the same element, with a particular number of neutrons (uranium 235 has 143 neutrons).

moderator Any substance in the reactor core that absorbs neutrons and slows down nuclear fission.

neutron A particle in the nucleus of atoms.

nucleus The central part of an atom.

ore A rock containing useful metals.

proton A particle found in the nucleus of atoms. The number of protons is balanced by the number of electrons.

PWR A pressurised water reactor. This uses water under high pressure as a coolant.

radiation Energy given out in waves by uranium and other radioactive substances as they decay.

radioactivity High-energy rays and particles given off by substances with unstable atoms, such as uranium.

reprocessing Spent fuel rods from nuclear reactors can be turned into fuel again and enriched for other reactors.

steam generator Also known as a heat exchanger. This takes the heat from the superhot coolant to produce steam in a separate tank of water, which drives turbines and generators.

turbine A machine with rotating blades.

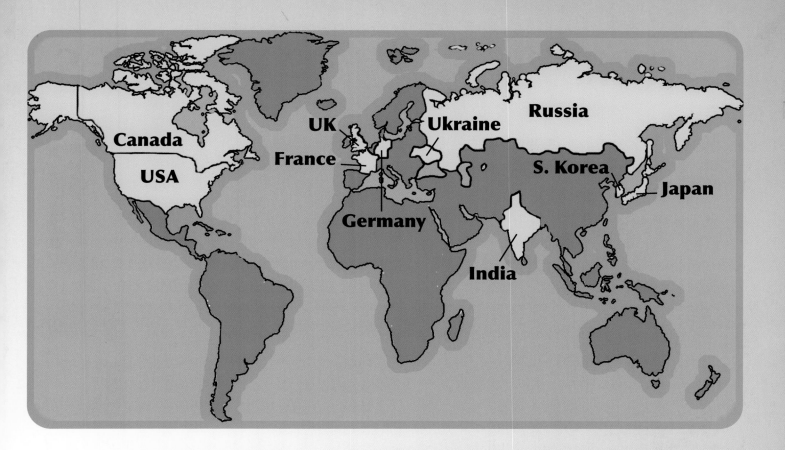

Useful Websites

If you're interested in finding out more about nuclear power, the following websites are helpful:

www.world-nuclear.org
www.nei.org
www.energysustained.com
www.iter.org
www.niauk.org
www.eia.doe.gov

Further Reading

World Issues: Energy Crisis by Ewan McLeish (Aladdin/Watts)
Issues in Our World: Energy Crisis by Ewan McLeish (Aladdin/Watts)
Your Environment: Future Energy by Sally Morgan (Aladdin/Watts)
Saving Our World: New Energy Sources by Nigel Hawkes (Aladdin/Watts)
Our World: Nuclear Power by Rob Bowden (Aladdin/Watts)
Energy Sources: Nuclear Power by Neil Morris (Franklin Watts)

Index

Photocredits

(Abbreviations: t – top, m – middle, b – bottom, l – left, r – right).

All photos istockphoto.com except: 3b, 20mr, 24tl: USNRC File Photo. 9tl: NATO. 10b: June 74 /dreamstime.com. 11bl: John Wollwerth/dreamstime.com. 14tl: iofoto/dreamstime.com. 15tl: courtesy of AMEC. 16tr: courtesy of CROCUS. 18-19: courtesy of AREVA. 21 both: courtesy SKB. 26t: courtesy of Nuclear Energy Institute. 26bl: courtesy ITER Organisation. 27ml: NASA.